I am woman
hear me draw

cartoons from the pen of Judy Horacek

NATIONAL
MUSEUM OF
AUSTRALIA
CANBERRA

A National Museum of Australia exhibition

© Cartoons by Judy Horacek

© National Museum of Australia 2002

National Museum of Australia
GPO Box 1901
Canberra ACT 2601
Phone +61 2 6208 5000
Fax +61 2 6208 5148
Email information@nma.gov.au
www.nma.gov.au

First published 2002
Reprinted 2003

National Library of Australia cataloguing-in-publication data
Horacek, Judy, 1961- .
I am woman, hear me draw.

ISBN 1 876944 10 2

1. Horacek, Judy, 1961 - Exhibitions.
2. Women - Caricatures and cartoons - Exhibitions.
3. Australian wit and humor, Pictorial - Exhibitions.
I. National Museum of Australia. II. Title.

741.5082

Designed and typeset by ROARcreative, Canberra
Printed by Goanna Print, Canberra

Foreword

The *Commonwealth Franchise Act 1902* effectively gave Australian women the vote. Like most political achievements, it was a complex blend of idealism and pragmatism and granted women the equally complex blessings of direct political involvement.

It is therefore particularly appropriate that this exhibition of Judy Horacek's characteristically wonderful, challenging, whimsical, hilarious and thoughtful cartoons about women's issues of all kinds should be held to commemorate the anniversary. I recommend them to you as a snapshot of where women are a hundred years on. Still fighting the battles — not for the vote, thank heavens, but for all the rest. I invite you to look, laugh and ponder.

Dawn Casey

Director

I am woman, hear me draw

Back in medieval times, a great debate raged as to whether women had souls. In more recent times, it was conceded that women did have souls, they just didn't have senses of humour. Since the advent of feminism, it's become more or less generally accepted that women have senses of humour, it's only feminists who don't. This is obviously progress.

I think one reason why women were supposed not to have senses of humour is that after a while we all got sick of laughing at the men's jokes and never being able to make our own. And the reason that feminists have been branded humourless is that we don't find jokes about the supposed stupidity of women or about violence against women particularly funny. Women, when they feature at all, are often the butt of traditional humour. Once you see things in a certain way, that is, from the point of view of the woman victim of the joke, you don't find quite a lot of jokes funny.

I call myself a feminist cartoonist, although I'm also interested in the environment and social justice. My work has always been concerned with women's experience, both the experience of 'women's things' and our experience of the world in general. Occasionally I've done a cartoon that women find hilarious and some men just don't get. One cartoon of mine shows a woman seated at a microphone with a man in a suit standing over her saying, 'If you could just try to sound less like a woman'. She replies, 'You want me to do animal impersonations?' I've seen straight couples nearly split up over this cartoon. I've also had the response from men, 'What, you're saying men sound like animals?' To me, and to the women who laugh at it — and even women who are quite conservative laugh at this cartoon — it's a wonderful expression of how our experience and our contribution is so often undervalued or silenced. We live in a world where to be told, 'You didn't do that like a woman' is supposed to be a compliment. If some men don't get this cartoon, well that pretty much proves its point. I think it means I'm doing my job.

I've claimed a lot of meaning for what is a fairly sparse line drawing. But that's what I love about cartooning — it is an incredibly simple medium capable of expressing great complexities. And not only that, it makes people laugh. I discovered cartooning shortly after I'd discovered feminism.

Cartooning seemed to me to be the perfect medium to express the new understanding that I now had of the world and my place in it. Cartoons were an ideal way to express my own point of view and my experience, to try to express women's shared experience, and to have my say about things that I felt strongly about.

To recap. What is now generally called first wave feminism happened around the turn of the century with women all over the world forming movements to demand the vote. Australia was the second nation in the world to give women the vote (New Zealand was first). Second wave feminism began in the 1960s and that's the wave we're still part of, unless we're now third wave or even post-feminists (this has been much discussed). What was originally called the Women's Liberation Movement (it became known as feminism later on) wanted equality for women on all levels. This encompassed demands for equal pay for equal work, equal opportunities, our right to control over our bodies, the right to abortion, an end to violence against women, the formation of refuges for victims of domestic violence, issues of sexuality, sexual harassment, childcare and more — a million things that were unjust and wrong about the way women were treated and their position in society. There were marches and anthems and slogans and posters and organising, a discovering of women's history and a flowering of artistic production.

The battle lines were fairly obvious in the 60s and 70s, becoming more complicated as time has gone on. (The so-called glass ceiling, for example, refers to the complicated and subtle set of factors that prevent a woman advancing in her career, something that is much more difficult to protest against than a law saying married women are not allowed to work.) Feminism has also had to realise that it cannot automatically speak for all women. Women of different classes, cultures and colours do not necessarily have the same issues as the white middle class feminists who mostly made up the vanguard of Women's Lib. The parameters of the movement have changed considerably over time. Feminism is now more properly called feminisms, to reflect the diversity of women's experiences and differing expectations of the movement.

In its far reaching impact on society and on people's thinking, feminism was arguably the most important social movement of the twentieth century.

Much of the initial change-the-world excitement and energy of the second wave was over by the time I went to uni. Many of the most glaring inequities had been at least partially rectified. As far as the women's movement went, I was in great danger of becoming one of those women who announce, 'I'm not a feminist, but...' Meaning that I knew I was as intelligent and capable as a man, and I expected to have the same rights and opportunities as men and wasn't that all there was to it? Somewhere in the back of my mind was the knowledge that many battles had been fought and that I was the beneficiary of the hard work and courage of the women who had fought those battles. But that was then and this was now, and hadn't everything been sorted out already?

Of course I couldn't fail to notice that most books were still by men, most pictures hanging in galleries were still by men, and nearly every single politician and decision maker was a man, but I figured that was just because women hadn't been quite good enough yet. An idea which contained the comforting thought that I would be one of the exceptions, I would be 'good enough'.

I was born in 1961 and I remember seeing women protesting on the television and in the newspapers from when I was quite young. Marches and rallies, the controversy over Germaine Greer's *The Female Eunuch*. I wasn't old enough to do anything much except swallow the media's line — that these women were aggressive and out of control, that women's libbers (as feminists were then known) were people to be avoided. Of course I believed that women should receive the same pay for the same work and

Woman drawing

Life on the Edge
Spinifex Press
1992

be allowed to keep working after marriage, and reproductive freedom and access to childcare seemed like good ideas, but did they have to be so unfeminine about it? (After forty years, and even though women's issues are now firmly on the mainstream agenda, the media is still running the same line.)

It wasn't until I had nearly finished my degree (majoring in Art History and English Literature because I kind of wanted to be an artist or a writer) that I chose to risk doing an essay on what I'd always thought of as 'the token feminist topic' on the list of essay topics (even though I half suspected it was a trap to test if you were really serious).

So I wrote an essay discussing Shakespeare's *Macbeth* and D H Lawrence's *Lady Chatterley's Lover* from a feminist perspective and I was changed forever. Once you discover sexual politics your life can never be the same. I realised that there was a whole lot more to the absence of women in public life than women not being quite good enough. Inequality and sexism were entrenched at every level, from personal relationships, to institutional structures, to what our society accepts as 'truth' and 'knowledge'. I became a huge fan of women's bookshops and women's publishing. I realised that even though an incredible amount had changed, the whole system still worked in favour of men. I realised that there was a lot of truth in slogans like 'To be considered as good as a man a woman has to be twice as good, fortunately this is not hard'. Okay it was corny and it had been around for years but I could now see the point.

And then I discovered cartooning. I was involved in a writing group and the leader of the group suggested we all wrote something and drew pictures to go with it. I'd always written and drawn, and I'd always read cartoons avidly, but somehow it had never really occurred to me to try cartooning. My first cartoon was about a family waking up one morning to discover a giant fish on their kitchen table which for some reason they can't get rid of. Parts of the page were three dimensional with liquid paper because I couldn't draw very well, and I had yet to discover the major cartooning technique of tracing, but I loved doing it. I realised that a cartoonist was what I really wanted to be.

And with my relatively new interest in feminism I had a whole subject area just crying out to be drawn. I soon discovered that I wasn't alone in this: along with more traditional art forms like painting, sculpture, writing and theatre, cartoons had been an important part of the women's movement for years. Women had also been making inroads into comedy, some very brave souls taking on the male bastion of stand-up which meant developing at least fifty comebacks to 'Show us your tits'. The fact that so many women were producing work, and the ideas that they expressed in the work itself reflected a new confidence in their own experience and their desire to change things.

I made the decision when I first began cartooning to nearly always draw women. After years of reading cartoons as a child I knew that women didn't really feature. There were the editorial cartoons in the mainstream dailies which were about daily political events in which women weren't involved, so of course they weren't in the cartoons. There were cartoons in magazines and books which occasionally showed a woman, but she was always an adjunct to the main male character — the sexy object of his desire or the overweight nag holding him back from his true path.

It made sense to me to people my cartoons with female characters. Obviously one would use a female character for a cartoon about mothering or period pain, but I used female characters in cartoons about everything — from occupational health and safety issues to existential dilemmas. Initially this risked the cartoon being misunderstood because some people couldn't see beyond the female character, they kept searching for the 'woman's issue' that they felt the cartoon must be about. But hell, women are over

50 per cent of the population, I figure that gives us some right to comment on the human condition.

It seems difficult to imagine now, but drawing cartoons about women and women's lives was quite a radical step. And making a woman the main character in cartoons about life in general was even more radical. I was nowhere near the first to do it, but it was still suspect when I started. Nowadays there are loads of women cartoonists doing cartoons about whatever they like. The mainstream media hasn't embraced many of us as yet, but women cartoonists are definitely out there on the fringes (and fridges), producing wonderful work at the community level and for alternative and independent publications.

A journalist once accused me of doing cartoons that were anti-men. I looked in surprise at the cartoons he was looking at. 'But there aren't any men in these cartoons', I said. 'Exactly', he said. We're not supposed to see the high level of violence against women in films, books and advertising as any sort of misogyny, but all you have to do is not put any men into your work and you're anti-male?

The little character that features in many of my cartoons is a kind of Everywoman. She is never necessarily the same person — I think it's important to draw women of different ages and different races and different sizes. Too many groups are rendered invisible by the dominant culture, and I want to redress this in my cartoons. One day I'll do a cartoon called 'Politically correct and proud of it'.

My characters aren't me. Some of the things that happen to them have happened to me, and we think similarly on most issues. But they are much more able to think of the perfect comeback at the exact moment they need it rather than hours later, like I do. It is very therapeutic to make cartoons in which you can be full of courage and possessed of a rapier-like wit. The figures I draw are all together much braver and sassier than I am, and quite possibly more politically astute. They are very capable of standing up for what they believe, and I can't help but admire them.

judy horacek

Sisters are doing it for themselves...

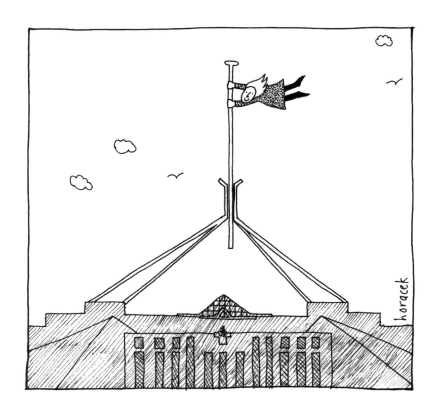

Woman on Parliament House

Everywoman's Guide to Getting into Parliament
Office of the Status of Women
1995

I am woman, hear me roar

Everywoman's Guide to Getting into Parliament
Office of the Status of Women
1995

Jack and Jill

Life on the Edge
Spinifex Press
1992

Mother Christmas

Christmas card
1991

Image consultant

Everywoman's Guide to Getting into Parliament
Office of the Status of Women
1995

Damn feminists

Women Against Violence
Centre Against Sexual Assault
November 1997

Animal impersonations

As I was Saying: The Wit and Wisdom of Australian Women
Five Mile Press
1992

It's a man's world...

Applications for first person

Woman with Altitude
Hyland House
1997

Photographing marbles

*An Illusory Image: A Report on the Media Coverage
and Portrayal of Women's Sport in Australia*
Australian Sports Commission
1997

Once they ruled the world

Alternative Law Journal
Legal Service Bulletin Co-op
June 1995

PATRIARCHY RULES

No 1 Non-Provocative Dressing

Providing you also lock yourself in a bank vault, this outfit is a 55% sure way to avoid being accused of inviting rape

No 2 Non-Provocative Behaviour

horacek

INVISIBILITY
or NON-EXISTENCE
Choose whichever is easier and/or more satisfying to you

Patriarchy rules

Reclaim the Night pamphlet
1988

Don't talk to strangers

Reclaim the Night pamphlet
1988

One small step

Woman with Altitude
Hyland House
1997

Building site

Unrequited Love Nos 1–100
McPhee Gribble
1994

Don't call me baby...

Things out of book

A Handle on Work
Council of Adult Education
1992

Cemetery of women

Age
10 May 1995

Birth of Venus

Unrequited Love Nos 1–100
McPhee Gribble
1994

Desert island

Unrequited Love Nos 1–100
McPhee Gribble
1994

Feminist man-haters

Body Jamming: Sexual Harassment, Feminism and Public Life
Random House
1997

These boots are made for walking...

Woman climbing mountain

The Women's Power Handbook
Penguin
1999

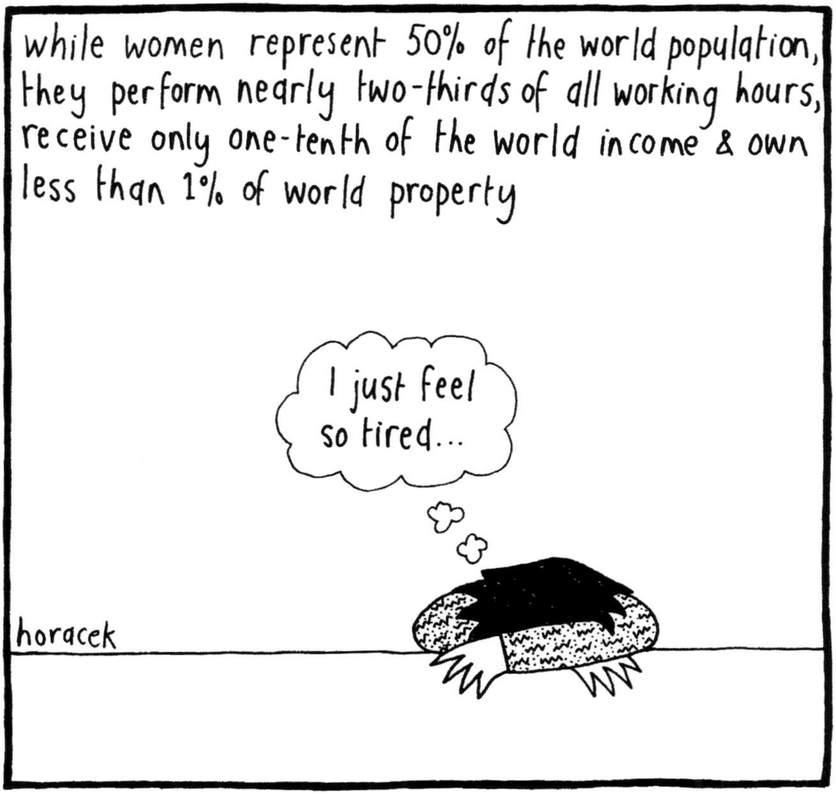

I just feel so tired
Unrequited Love Nos 1–100
McPhee Gribble
1994

888

Centre for Labour Research campaign
1995

Feminist insomnia

Women Against Violence
Centre Against Sexual Assault
June 1997

Paid maternity leave

Alternative Law Journal
Legal Service Bulletin Co-op
October 1996

Share childcare

Christmas card
1991

So many stairs

Law Handbook
Redfern Legal Centre Publishing
1999

The legal system

Law Handbook
Redfern Legal Centre Publishing
1999

Privatisation fairy

Victorian Trades Hall campaign
1995

Global warming

Weekend Australian Magazine
12 May 2001

Career advice no. 34

Age
1996

Working 9 to 5 (and the rest)...

Cuckoo cuckoo

APESMA Work Survival Guide
Association of Professional Engineers, Scientists and Managers
August 2001

Can't urinate standing up

Woman with Altitude
Hyland House
1997

Woman into pool

Everywoman's Guide to Getting into Parliament
Office of the Status of Women
1995

Dr Jekyll

Greeting card
1991

Money money money

New Woman
July 1995

Agenda items 3 to 15

Centre for Labour Research campaign
1995

Career advice no. 9

Everywoman's Guide to Getting into Parliament
Office of the Status of Women
1995

Career advice no. 41

Weekend Australian Magazine
17 April 1999

Career advice no. 23

Weekend Australian Magazine
29 June 1998